Snap books®

STAR BIOGRAPHIES

Daniel Radcliffe

by Sheila Griffin Llanas

CAPSTONE PRESS
a capstone imprint

Snap Books are published by Capstone Press,
151 Good Counsel Drive, P.O. Box 669, Mankato, Minnesota 56002.
www.capstonepress.com

092009
005618CGS10

Library of Congress Cataloging-in-Publication Data
Llanas, Sheila Griffin.
    Daniel Radcliffe / by Sheila Griffin Llanas.
    p. cm. — (Snap books. Star biographies)
    Summary: "Describes the life and career of Daniel Radcliffe" — Provided by publisher.
    Includes bibliographical references and index.
    ISBN 978-1-4296-4723-6 (library binding)
    1. Radcliffe, Daniel, 1989– — Juvenile literature. 2. Actors — Great Britain —
Biography — Juvenile literature. I. Title. II. Series.
PN2598.R27L43 2010
791.4302'8092 — dc22   2009035104
[B]

Editor: Jennifer Besel
Designer: Ashlee Suker
Media Researcher: Marcie Spence
Production Specialist: Laura Manthe

Photo Credits:
Getty Images Inc./Bruce Glikas/FilmMagic, 28; Ferdaus Shamim/WireImage, 5; Gareth Davies, 18;
    Jim Spellman/WireImage, cover;
Globe Photos, 9
Landov LLC/CBS/John Paul Filo, 19
Newscom, 14; AFP Photo/Leon Neal, 6; Ari Mintz, 23; Darla Khazei, CelebrityHomePhotos, 24;
    Flashburst/WENN, 27; Frances M. Roberts, 15; uppa/IPOL, 13; Warner Bros./Close, Murray, 20
Rex USA/Carl de Souza, 17
Supplied by Capital Pictures, 11, 25

Essential content terms are bold and are defined at the bottom of the page where they first appear.

Table of Contents

Walking the Red Carpet

It was pouring rain as Daniel Radcliffe leapt from the back of a silver car. More than 3,000 screaming fans lined the streets of Leicester Square in London. Cameras flashed. Reporters shouted questions. It was July 7, 2009. The face of the famous wizard had just arrived for the world **premiere** of *Harry Potter and the Half-Blood Prince*.

Dan, as friends call him, was no stranger to the red carpet. This was the sixth movie in the incredibly popular *Harry Potter* series. He stepped into the downpour without an umbrella. His metallic gray suit, coral shirt, and paisley tie got soaking wet. But Dan smiled and greeted hundreds of fans. He signed books, posters, and photographs.

Emma Watson, who plays Hermione Granger, looked lovely in a vintage dress by 1970s designer Ossie Clark. Rupert Grint, who plays Ron Weasley, looked dapper in a fitted black suit. The three posed for photos. Dan's two costars are like siblings to him.

premiere — the first public showing of a film

Dan didn't seem to mind the pouring rain at the premiere of *Harry Potter and the Half-Blood Prince*.

Dan, Emma, and Rupert talked to reporters and fans in the pouring rain. Some celebrities would have run from the downpour. But Dan and his costars knew fans had waited for hours to get a glimpse of them. They gave the fans what they wanted.

Finally the film was about to start. It would be played in both the Odeon and Empire theaters at the same time. Dan and the others dashed into the Odeon theater, soaking wet and grinning from ear to ear. This was Dan's sixth time walking the red carpet for a *Harry Potter* premiere. Each premiere seemed bigger than the last. This time, he was 19, not the 12-year-old boy who first walked the red carpet. He had grown up a lot. And he had become one of the most famous young actors in the world.

Rupert Grint, Emma Watson, and Dan posed for pictures even though they looked a little soggy.

A Potter Cheat Sheet

By the end of the series, Dan will have starred in eight major films playing the part of Harry Potter. In fact, he will have spent half his life as author J. K. Rowling's boy wizard. It can be a bit tricky to keep all the movies straight. Here's a list of the movies for your reference.

1. *Harry Potter and the Sorcerer's Stone* was released on November 16, 2001, when Dan was 12 years old. In the film, Harry learns he is a wizard and begins his adventures at Hogwarts.

2. *Harry Potter and the Chamber of Secrets* was released November 15, 2002, when Dan was 13 years old. Together, Harry, Ron, and Hermione investigate the sinister events at Hogwarts linked to the mysterious Chamber of Secrets.

3. *Harry Potter and the Prisoner of Azkaban* was released June 4, 2004. In this movie, Dan explores new dangers for Harry that change the character's life forever.

4. *Harry Potter and the Goblet of Fire* was released November 18, 2005, when Dan was 16. Harry is forced to compete in a wizards' tournament, which leads to Voldemort's return.

5. *Harry Potter and the Order of the Phoenix* was released on July 11, 2007. The wizard world is reluctant to believe Harry's claim that Voldemort has returned.

6. *Harry Potter and the Half-Blood Prince* was released July 15, 2009, when Dan was 19. Dumbledore and Harry embark on a deadly journey that may reveal how to defeat Lord Voldemort.

7. *Harry Potter and the Deathly Hallows: Part 1* is scheduled to be released November 19, 2010. Harry, Ron, and Hermione take off on a quest to bring down the dark lord.

8. *Harry Potter and the Deathly Hallows: Part 2* is scheduled for release July 15, 2011, just eight days before Dan's 22nd birthday. In this movie, Harry meets Voldemort for their final showdown.

CHAPTER 2

A London Childhood

Daniel Jacob Radcliffe was born on July 23, 1989, in London, England. Dan grew up in Fulham, a London neighborhood. His mother, Marcia Gresham Radcliffe, is a **casting director**. His father, Alan Radcliffe, is a **literary agent**. Dan is their only child. The Radcliffes share their home with two border terrier dogs, Binka and Nugget.

Dan had a happy home life with his parents. On car trips, the Radcliffe family listened to Broadway show tunes. The three of them often went to see plays together.

At age 5, Dan had a small part in a play where he was a monkey. Afterward, he declared he wanted to be an actor when he grew up. As a casting director, Dan's mother saw many hopeful actors get rejected. She knew that show business could be rough. She hoped an acting career wasn't in Dan's future.

casting director — the person in charge of finding actors for a play
literary agent — someone who helps authors get their books published

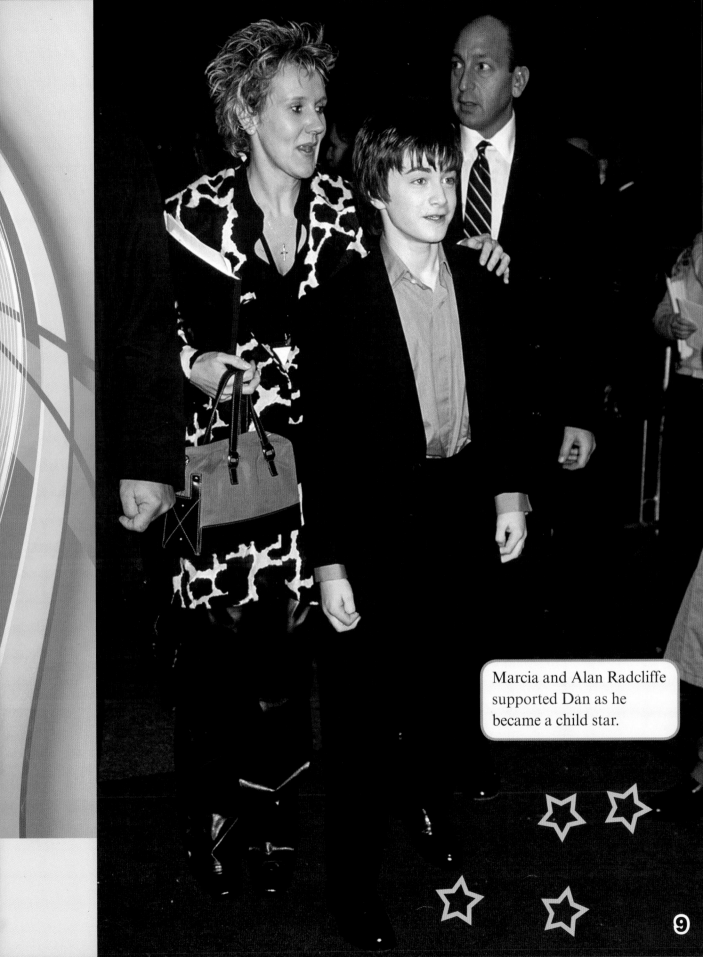

Marcia and Alan Radcliffe supported Dan as he became a child star.

A Not-So-Great Student

School was rough for Dan. He attended Sussex House, a private boys' school in London. Later he went to the City of London school, another top boys' school. He had good friends, but he struggled with schoolwork. Sports skills didn't come naturally for Dan, either. At school, Dan was frustrated and had low self-esteem. By age 8, he really thought he was no good at anything. It made him depressed. His mother praised his social skills. But Dan didn't think that was worth much.

"The thing is at school I was rubbish at sports, and I was not particularly academic at all."
— Dan speaking about school life in an interview with Australian TV program *ACA*.

Overcoming Obstacles

Dan has a learning disability that makes academics and sports difficult. Dan has a mild form of **dyspraxia**, a condition that affects the brain. A person with dyspraxia has trouble with hand and eye coordination. It is hard for Dan to ride a bicycle and swim, though you wouldn't know it from his *Harry Potter* stunts. It is even hard for him to write. When he goes to set his pen on paper, he can't tell where the pen will land. As a boy, Dan learned to deal with his dyspraxia. Playing video games improved his coordination. But he still has a bit of trouble tying his shoelaces.

dyspraxia — a disability that makes it hard to make coordinated movements

A Big Boost of Confidence

Dan's parents told their friends about Dan's low self-esteem. Sue Latimer was an **agent** who had gone to acting school with Dan's father. She suggested Dan **audition** for an acting job. Producers were casting for the BBC movie *David Copperfield*. Dan's parents wondered if trying out for a part would boost his confidence. Even if he didn't get the part, he would have a good story to tell his classmates. So 9-year-old Dan tried out to play the main character, young David Copperfield. He competed against hundreds of boys. To everyone's surprise, Dan landed the role.

Young Dan starred in *David Copperfield* with actor Bob Hoskins.

To Dan, acting itself was more exciting than the audition. Dan loved acting. He had a lot of fun on set. And his self-confidence soared. Dan finally felt like he was good at something.

Dan starred in the TV movie with acting legends Bob Hoskins, Maggie Smith, and Ian McKellen. *David Copperfield* was shown on TV in England on Christmas Day in 1999. The movie later played in the United States on PBS. *David Copperfield* was a huge success. Dan had found his skill.

agent — someone who helps actors find work

audition — to try out for an acting role

Destined for Stardom

After *David Copperfield*, Dan's acting career took off. Sue Latimer became Dan's agent. In 2000, Dan landed his next role in a Hollywood movie called *The Tailor of Panama*. In this spy thriller, he played Mark Pendel, the son of a tailor. It was a small part, but he acted with Pierce Brosnan, a former *James Bond* star. Dan's on-screen dad was Geoffrey Rush and his movie mom was Jamie Lee Curtis. One day, Jamie Lee looked at Dan and told Dan's mother, "He could be Harry Potter." No one knew then how true her remark would turn out to be!

The Right Face at the Right Time

At the same time that Dan was filming *The Tailor of Panama*, producers were looking for a boy to play Harry Potter. More than 16,000 boys had auditioned for the role. But none of them were right for the part. The producers were getting worried. Who would be perfect enough to play such an important character?

One night at a play, Dan and his parents happened to sit behind David Heyman and Steve Kloves. The men were the producer and writer for the first *Harry Potter* movie. Dan's parents knew them from their work. The two men stared at Dan. Dan looked like the boy on the cover of J. K. Rowling's book. He was the right age. David and Steve had seen *David Copperfield*. They knew Dan had acting experience.

Producer David Heyman (back left) and director Chris Columbus (back right) were thrilled with their young cast.

David and Steve barely watched the play that evening. They were too excited. They just might have found their Harry Potter! During intermission, David asked Dan to audition for the role.

Dan's parents worried that their son would suffer rejection. The chances of Dan getting the part were slim. Why put him through the pain? They were not sure Dan should audition. As for Dan, he was excited at the possibility of playing such an important part. But he was willing to accept whatever decision his parents made.

Audiences were thrilled with Dan's performance in *Harry Potter and the Sorcerer's Stone.*

The Role of a Lifetime

The next morning, Dan's parents decided to let him audition for the part of Harry Potter. His parents spoke with David Heyman first. They wanted to make sure Dan would be protected from the media if he got the part. David assured Dan's parents that Dan would be safe. So the Radcliffes agreed to let him try out.

Dan nervously walked into the audition room. He acted a scene with a boy trying out for the part of Neville. Then he read a scene with the director, Chris Columbus. But Chris did not read the lines in the script. He made up new lines. He mixed things up to see if Dan could **improvise**. Dan made a very good impression.

"I felt very nervous because I knew that I was about to step into a room with a very famous director. But I didn't feel pressured because I didn't expect to get the part."
— Dan in an interview for *Masterpiece Theater* on PBS.

improvise — to make up material on the spot

Dan did not have to wait long to learn his fate. The day after his audition, the phone rang while Dan was taking a bath. His dad answered the phone and took the message that would change Dan's life forever. He had gotten the part! Dan would bring Harry Potter to life on the big screen.

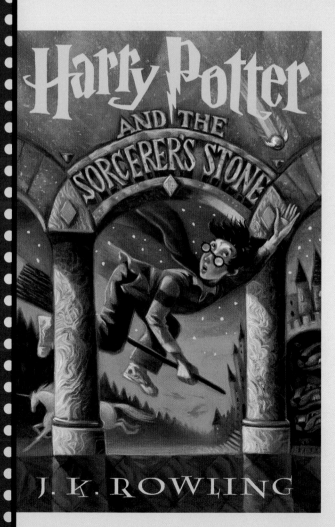

Reading Up

Dan credits J. K. Rowling with turning him into a reader. He partially read the first two books when he was 8. But he admits he was not a big reader at the time. As soon as he got the part of Harry Potter, Dan decided to read the first book again. He ended up reading the first four books back-to-back. His favorite book is *The Chamber of Secrets*. Even the boy who plays Harry Potter is a fan of the books!

Just as Dan loved the books, J. K. Rowling loved the choice of Dan to play her main character. The director showed her Dan's screen test. She knew he was just right for the part.

CHAPTER 3

Becoming Harry Potter

Dan spent a year filming *Harry Potter and the Sorcerer's Stone*. Starting in September 2000, a studio car picked Dan up at his house at 7:30 each morning. Dan's father quit his job so he could be on set with his son every day. At Leavesden Studios in Watford, England, elaborate sets were created for the movie. In makeup, Dan had Harry's famous lightning bolt applied to his forehead.

At the studio, Dan had his own dressing room, with a kitchen, bedroom, and living room. During downtime, he watched TV, made a sandwich, or rested. On breaks, Dan relaxed by playing PlayStation games and watching movies. Dan spent three to five hours a day with a tutor. He studied history, math, religion, and French. Dan also had to memorize his lines. And he had a lot of lines. As the main character, Harry Potter has lines in nearly every scene of the movie. When he got home at 7:30 at night, he ate supper, watched TV, and went to bed early.

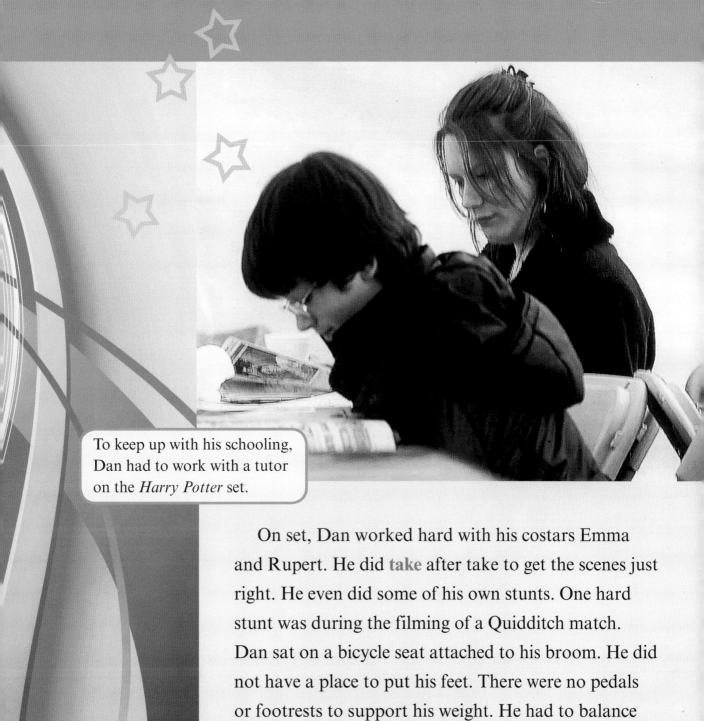

To keep up with his schooling, Dan had to work with a tutor on the *Harry Potter* set.

On set, Dan worked hard with his costars Emma and Rupert. He did **take** after take to get the scenes just right. He even did some of his own stunts. One hard stunt was during the filming of a Quidditch match. Dan sat on a bicycle seat attached to his broom. He did not have a place to put his feet. There were no pedals or footrests to support his weight. He had to balance himself as he was lifted by a hydraulic rig. The rig pulled him 22 feet (7 meters) into the air. Sitting on the broom was painful and challenging to hold onto.

take — a scene filmed at one time without stopping the camera

In the Spotlight

The first *Harry Potter* movie premiered on November 4, 2001. Celebs like Sarah Ferguson, Duchess of York, Ben Stiller, Sting, and Cher came for the huge event. But the star of the night was Dan. Fans screamed his name. Reporters snapped his picture. The flashing cameras were as bright as strobe lights. Dan was nervous, but the poised 12-year-old didn't show his fear. He smiled and waved. He posed for pictures and spoke to reporters.

Daniel Radcliffe soon became a household name as the media praised the young boy's work in the film. He appeared on big-name TV talk shows with Oprah and David Letterman.

Harry Potter author, J. K. Rowling, posed for pictures with Dan and his costars at the first movie premiere.

Dan has made several appearances on David Letterman's show to promote his movies.

When Dan went out in public, fans mobbed him on the street. He saw his face on a bus. He even saw a Lego version of himself. At first, it seemed unreal. But Dan accepted it all cheerfully. He greeted fans with a smile and signed autographs whenever possible.

But Dan tried to keep his privacy too. When Dan went out, he pulled his baseball cap over his eyes and tried not to attract attention. When he visited New York for the U. S. premiere, he acted like a regular tourist. He went to the top of the Empire State Building. He shopped at the famous toy store FAO Schwartz and bought a magic set. Dan didn't let fame go to his head. His life as a star was just beginning.

Dan does many of his own stunts in the *Harry Potter* movies.

Growing Up on Set

Dan didn't have time to let fame go to his head. He went to work on the second *Potter* movie just three days after the first film premiered. *The Chamber of Secrets* was more intense with duels and advanced stunts. And so it went with all the movies. On and off for eight years, Dan explored many deep emotions in the role of Harry. He lost loved ones and fell in love. With each movie, Dan became a better actor. Scenes that once needed nine takes **wrapped** in three.

wrap — to finish filming

As Harry grew up, so did Dan. His voice deepened. He grew more confident. But fortunately, Dan didn't get much taller. A huge growth spurt would have meant the end of his run as Harry. Today Dan is only 5 feet, 6 inches (1.7 meters) tall. He credits his mother with his short height. His mom is only 5 feet (1.5 meters) tall.

Dan's costars grew up on set too. Dan is close with Rupert and Emma. He's also good friends offscreen with Tom Felton, who plays Harry's enemy Draco Malfoy. The young actors all had to deal with the pressure of fame. And they all had to do homework between scenes. But they had each other to lean on.

Dan's adult *Harry Potter* costars were great role models. During filming of *The Prisoner of Azkaban*, Dan became good friends with Gary Oldman. Oldman starred as Sirius Black. Dan said he did some of his best scenes with Gary.

Stunts

Dan performed some challenging stunts in the *Harry Potter* movies. He learned to scuba dive for the Tri-Wizard Tournament. In another scene, Dan battled a dragon. In one part, he actually jumped off a rocky cliff with a 50-foot (15-meter) drop.

But some stunts in the films were too dangerous for Dan to do himself. Stunt double David Holmes did some of the stunts in place of Dan. David looks quite a bit like Dan, but you'll only see David from the back or side in the movies.

CHAPTER 4

Life Outside Hogwarts

For six years, Dan dedicated himself to the role of Harry Potter. But the cast and crew got a much needed break between the fourth and fifth movies. Dan didn't take a vacation, though. He took the opportunity to expand his acting skills.

Dan Takes the Stage

In early 2007, Dan tackled something he hadn't done since he was 5 years old. He acted onstage. Dan landed the lead role in a play called *Equus*. Dan's character, Alan Strang, had an unhealthy interest in horses. Dan liked the challenge of the stage. As a stage actor, Dan had to project his voice. He trained for 18 months with a vocal coach. He learned to speak up and say his lines clearly. The intense role also required Dan to appear naked onstage for a few minutes every night. At first, some people were shocked. But for Dan, it was just part of his job.

"If you take the job, you take everything with it. It's never going to be the most comfortable, natural place to be naked, with an audience."

— Dan speaking about his role in *Equus* in an interview on *Inside the Actors Studio*.

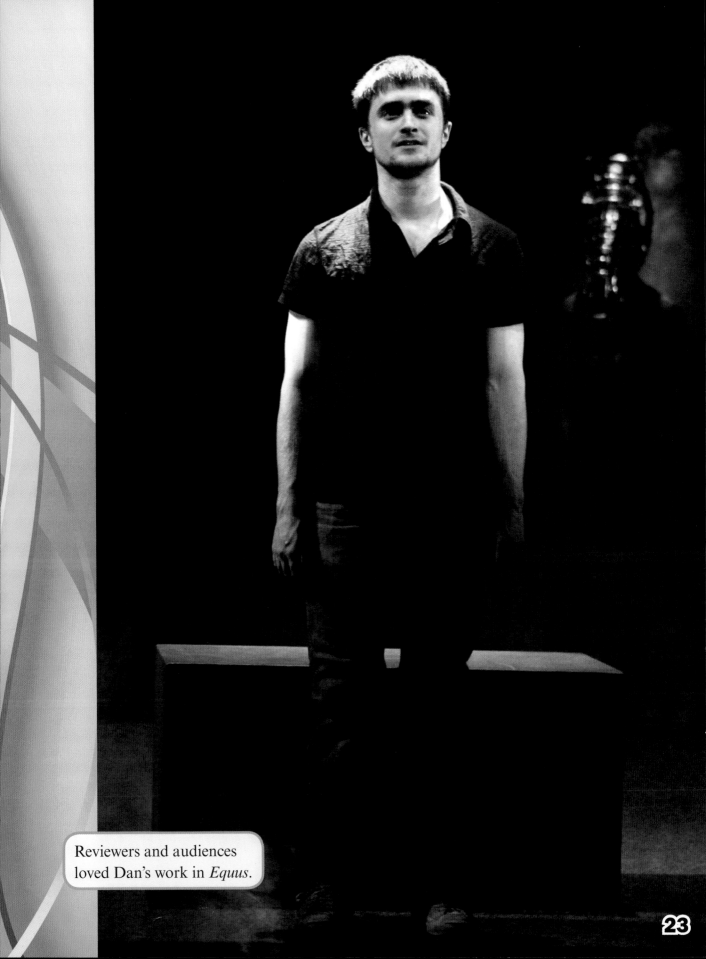

Reviewers and audiences loved Dan's work in *Equus*.

Equus opened on February 27, 2007, at the Gielgud Theatre in London's West End. On opening night, Dan was filled with doubt. What if he forgot his lines? What if nobody liked the play? He didn't need to worry. The cast got a standing ovation. Over four months, Dan performed the role of Alan 128 times. Working onstage helped Dan's acting. He learned to be more focused and professional. He also gained **stamina** from the pressure of doing a show every night.

Equus was such a hit that the cast was asked to perform in the United States. Dan made his Broadway debut in September 2008. Dan bought a gorgeous three-bedroom apartment in Manhattan. He lived there while he performed in New York. He still owns the apartment, so he can use it when he travels to the states.

Dan paid $4.9 million for an apartment in this Manhattan building.

stamina — the energy to keep doing something for a long time

In *December Boys*, Dan (middle) played the oldest of four orphans on a life-changing vacation.

More Movies

Between the London and U.S. runs of *Equus*, Dan starred in a film called *December Boys*. In the movie, Dan plays Maps, the oldest of four orphans on a vacation in Australia's outback. Unlike Harry Potter, Maps was a quiet character. Dan liked the challenge of communicating with less dialogue. For the movie, he trained to perfect an Australian accent. He also did his first onscreen kiss with costar Teresa Palmer.

After *December Boys*, Dan also starred in a British TV film for Masterpiece Theater. *My Boy Jack* is a true story about World War I. Dan played Jack, a 17-year-old soldier, who was killed in battle. As he acted in the realistic battle scenes, Dan got an idea of what it would be like to fight in a war.

CHAPTER 5

A Life of Fame and Fortune

Dan has become one of the world's most famous stars. As early as 2004, Dan was already the second richest teen in England. In 2008, Dan and Miley Cyrus tied for the number one spot on *Forbes Magazine's* list of richest tweens. In 2008 alone, he made $25 million.

Dan donates money to many charities. He gives to Demelza House Children's Hospice. This organization helps terminally ill children. He also gave a donation to the Trevor Project, a suicide prevention hotline for gay teenagers.

All his money and stardom has a downside. **Paparazzi** flock wherever Dan goes. But he takes this inconvenience in stride. During his role in *Equus*, Dan figured out a way to fool the paparazzi. Every night, he wore the same jacket and hat. That way, every photo looked like it was taken on the same day.

paparazzi — aggressive photographers who take pictures of celebrities

During the London run of *Equus*, Dan wore the same black jacket and green hat each night to fool photographers.

The Life of Dan

Even though he's famous, Dan is a down-to-earth guy. He prefers jeans and T-shirts to glamorous suits. He eats pizza, hangs out with friends, and plays video games. He cooks microwave meals like macaroni and cheese. Dan relaxes by watching *The Simpsons* and *SpongeBob SquarePants*. And he is a big fan of cricket and American football. He keeps up on current music trends and also loves classic rock and roll. His favorite bands include Nirvana, The Clash, and the Red Hot Chili Peppers.

With his amazing acting talent and magical smile, Dan is a superstar all around the world.

Dan keeps his personal life private. He dated Laura O'Toole, his *Equus* costar, for a while. When he has a girlfriend, he likes to protect her from the spotlight.

Dan now has his own apartment near his parents' home in Fulham. In his spare time, Dan collects art and reads. He also writes poetry. He has even published some poems under the pen name Jacob Gershon.

Still to Come

After a decade on the Hogwarts set, Dan was ready to move on. In 2009, Dan signed on to play photographer Dan Eldon in a movie called *The Journey Is the Destination*. The movie is scheduled to show in theaters in 2011.

Dan is learning new skills so he'll be ready for any part that comes his way. He takes ballet lessons in case he is offered a part in a dance musical. He's also taking singing lessons. He would like to act in another Broadway play. And he hopes to direct a movie one day.

Daniel Radcliffe will always be connected to Harry Potter. But this rising star has high hopes for his future, and so do his fans. Fans around the world are eager to see where this A-lister will go next.

"To be honest, I'm never happier than when I'm on a film set. That's a long way to tell you that I want to keep working."
— Dan in an interview with *IF Magazine*.

Glossary

agent (AY-juhnt) — someone who helps actors find work

audition (aw-DISH-uhn) — a tryout performance for an actor

casting director (KAST-ing duh-REK-tur) — the person in charge of finding actors for a play or movie

dyspraxia (dis-PRAK-see-uh) — a motor learning disability that makes it hard for a person to make smooth and coordinated movements

improvise (IM-pruh-vize) — to make up material on the spot

literary agent (LIT-uh-rer-ee AY-juhnt) — someone who helps authors sell and publish books

paparazzi (pah-puh-RAHT-see) — aggressive photographers who take pictures of celebrities for sale to magazines or newspapers

premiere (pruh-MIHR) — the first public performance of a film, play, or work of music or dance

stamina (STAM-uh-nuh) — the energy and strength to keep doing something for a long time

take (TAYK) — a scene filmed at one time without stopping the camera

wrap (RAP) — slang word for finishing a scene or production of a movie

Read More

Dougherty, Terri. *Daniel Radcliffe.* People in the News. Detroit: Lucent Books, 2009.

Jones, Jen. *Being Famous.* 10 Things You Need to Know About. Mankato, Minn.: Capstone Press, 2008.

Rawson, Katherine. *Daniel Radcliffe.* Kid Stars! New York: PowerKids Press, 2010.

Watson, Stephanie. *Daniel Radcliffe: Film and Stage Star.* Hot Celebrity Biographies. Berkeley Heights, N.J.: Enslow, 2009.

Internet Sites

FactHound offers a safe, fun way to find Internet sites related to this book. All of the sites on FactHound have been researched by our staff.

Here's all you do:

Visit *www.facthound.com*

FactHound will fetch the best sites for you!

Index